AF257855

The Owl Hymns

Poems for Monsters and Madmen

William F. Burk

Copyright © 2026 by William F. Burk

All rights reserved.

No portion of this book may be reproduced in any form without written permission from the publisher or author, except as permitted by U.S. copyright law.

To my grandmother, Glennice.

Introduction

I did not intend to publish another poetry volume after finishing my second one, *The Dove Curses.* I assume that was simply an ignorant assumption, given that poems are mercurial things and often come and go as they please. In that way, I suppose that I will never exhaust them. In this volume, I encountered abstractions, perspectives on both beauty and trauma. It is here that I learned that the line between monster and madman is all but rather thin.

This volume is a more adequate example of the Abstractist form. Poems featured focus less on narrative and more on awareness, feeling existence rather than describing it, and the human soul in relation to the cosmos. Enjoy.

William F. Burk

Contents

the songs that set us free

I heard you

Cry that night

As we swam,

And the sun

Set behind the

Ephemeral sea...

We were

Children

Once, and

We could

Not see,

But older we

Are now, lost

In that ephemeral

Sea, as you

Cry to me,

And I hold you

As we sing

And sway upon

The waves

Of that ephemeral

Sea, knowing soon

The storm will

Cease in the songs

That set us free.

Note: Yanmar 2024

Office walls,

As light flows in

The windows and

I dream of times

And futures

When, to □□□(New Genesis)

And sing that song

To find that I've

Been here all

Along—but don't know

When or how long

It's been, but

Life goes on

And we must agree

That for the time being,

You were good to me.

Put Us All to Rest

Lively still

Beyond the

Veil, we see with

Eyes—unfurled.

With rambling cause

And bygone all

We see the bird

Take wing.

O, over the sea

Where can it be

That one sought

Til' he was lost?

And sang to us,

A joyful song

And put us all to rest.

He Clothes Us In Blue

The flower

Of the field

Doused in blue

Sway singing

In sounds of

Sorrow, where

One might see

And one might

Hear, a cacophony

Of sweets that

We hold dear.

O blue O blue

I sing your song

Light a star

A billion miles away

Long long gone,

But your gown

Azure I see it

Now, and feel it I do,

Comfort I see,

I feel it in my heart

That there is understanding

Between you and

Me. That God clothes

You, and does not

Forget, that fear and

Anxiety plague us

Yet. But he clothes the

Lily, and now I see,

That in that there

Is understanding between

The sorrow of

You and me.

Jonah In The Dreads

Lightning strikes

Twice but does not

Save face underneath

A golden sea.

I sit here, in

Waves that dread

To swallow me.

Jonah, Jonah,

What ever did you

See? Swallowed whole

Did the the fish

Seem to love the

Lost or was he sent

For other means.

O, Lord! O, Lord!

I swim in this lengthy

Sea. I fear, I fear, that

It dreads to swallow me.

The Beast Destroys; The Beast He Loves You So

The beast fixes

The beast destroys

He sits alone and sees

What he has sewn

A cocoon of death

I see it there,

But born it with be

And destroy all that

Is here.

I love you dear

You love the beast

But tries to tame him

Fall on deaf ears

So we sit

Here, lonesome

Among rubble

And we wonder

If we shall ever

Again be

Lovers.

Anniversary Poem//Loathing Dirges

You are my muse

My peaceful sea

Deep blue bond

Pure and tenderly,

Oh I love you

Yes I do, for times

Of strife and tranquility

Too. You are my

Love, my longing

Pursuit, for your

Heart, your hand

Over and over

Again.

Forevermore,

The tides will sway,

Yet in those blue eyes

My heart will stay, for

I love you, Mandi,

Today, tomorrow,

and yesterday.

Happy anniversary.

Therapy Session

I live in an act,

and I don't know who

I am. I am left with myself,

I am left with a beast, I quite

hate myself, lost in

Darkened despair; I've been

defensive my whole life,

And I fear that either

I feel like a good person, yet

when she's upset,

I am a bad person,

I am a bipolar painting,

Lost by Van Gogh, and the

Only one who words me so

Seeks me as Poe, for

I'm afraid that I am

a bad person, hear the

Beating of the heart

(mean) (combative)

Remnants of my

Past. I've had to fight

for myself, so love

Is odd, I sit here now

And destroy it, that

Love, before my very eyes

Am I a lost cause,

Filled with rage and lies?

The Tree Lamentation

The trees

Are gone

And I miss

Them so, on

Mountaintops

Vain, merry

And low.

I miss the

Trees, and

They have left

Under baskets

Weaved with

Sin and theft

And the trees

They are no

More, caught

In life's grisly

Score, of trumpets,

It longs for trumpets,

For loss and yearn

The years of final

From it.

It seeks, it soothes,

Over time, it grows

Again.

The trees are

Gone, and I

Miss them so.

I return to that place,

Where none should go,

And speak to the springs,

As each droplet flows,

I miss you, trees,

Wherever did you go?

The world is quiet

And gray now

I miss you, trees,

Wherever did you go?

Gone with time,

Imagination too...

Oh dearest shrine

Or cathedral of nature so...

I miss you, trees,

Wherever did you go?

Hour By Hour, Fight After Fight

I love you

Ever more

Day by day

As minutes transpire

Oh do I love you

Hour by hour.

Fight after fight

Oh I love you still

As minutes transpire

Day by day

Ever more

Oh do I love you so.

A Bird Named Free

I caught

A bird

And named her

Free.

And over

Time, she

Loved me.

But lost the joy

And caged

Became she

So did she

Beat her wings

And desire to

Be free, for

She deigned

For love, and

I tried to give

Yet tarnished

I was, and golden

Was she. She, named

Free, stayed here

In this cage with me

And O did I love

Her, as she stayed

Here with me,

But O did I fail

To love this bird

Named Free

And O did I love

This bird named

Free. I will try

Again, which

Each new day,

To love she rightly,

This bird named Free.

The Painful Poem

A fire burns

In your heart

For me, and

I do not know

Why

But through

It all, smiles

And Tears, I can

Now see past

My lie.

That my

Heart is

Precious and

Lovable, and

You hold it dear

And your love

For me, so

Soft and sweet

Does all to

Break my fear.

Pain Beyond Distance

I don't sleep

I don't sing

I hear the voices

Sadly, cacophony

Deadly sad, I

See gray that

Fades to black

And sits upon

A throne

Undone, with

Distaste, you

See me, but

At last I see me

Falling as the

Whale does swallow

Me. How you loved me,

Do you still, as I

Sit upon the

Windowsill.

The ground is far away

But for you to loath me

Is pain beyond distance.

Of Monsters and Madmen

Love

Is, a word—

An incessant

Howl that

Falls here and

There in a kind

Of roundabout, as

We see it

Tortured, we

See it proved—

But do we see

It here, between me

And you? Lost among,

The weeds of

Life, I cannot

See the end with

This pair of eyes—

Please dear! Please!

Love me still when

I am a monster and

I cannot see ahead—

Lost in my mind,

Lost in my chest,

I merely wanted to

Give you all I could—

But now I see, as

The mirror pieces

Back together, that

I'm in nothingness now

And I may never get better.

Not the Owl Hymn

Am I more

Concerned with

Who I am than

Who I need to be?

Do I sit between

An owl's hymn,

And the nightingale

Who sings to me?

Oh, I forget what

I forget, and say

That I am wrong

But I tell the owl

Of who I am and heed

The nightingale's song

To one, to all

A mirror's

Fall, of grace and

Shattered naught.

For we see what they

See, but what they

See, are but lies disguised

As hawks.

And does the visage

I see before me

Sing of good and gold

For left in me are naught

But here, the lies and

Wrongs wrought old.

I love you dear,

I see you dear,

Please give me that

Time of day. It's

Evening now, and

The night is near,

Too late when the

Frost will stray.

I sit here now

And watch the sun,

Sink low with hopes

And dreams

Of a dying man

And his dying plan—

Selfish indeed.

My darling dear,

I will heed my

wrongs, and stray

Before Night's fall,

I sit here now, and hear

No more, as I sing

This owl's song.

Johnny Looks Like A Movie Star

A picture sits

Upon the casket—

(Johnny looks like a

Movie star.)

A simple man—

And down-to-earth,

A quiet and silly

Soul.

Ricky stands upon

The stage

With a brown

Guitar. Amazing grace—

It fills the room

As we stare at the

Flag that covers

The casket—

A voice so low,

As Ricky sings the bass

"Sing, Ricky!"

Sing with soul,

Upon that brown

Guitar...

The family sits, and

Weeps to God:

"Amazing Grace! Amazing Grace!"

His photo looks like

A movie star.

Light Within (A Fragmentary Passage)

A sky, a

Scene—

In brilliant

Gray and green,

Dazzled, that

Brings the heart

To break the

Soul, and let

The light shine

In—

O, let the

Light blaze

Within—

Angel (A Dirge)

If I

Could go

To the steps

Of that church—

To the rise of

That street, to

Talk to you—

You, seven-year-

Old—

Oh, the things

I'd say,

Like don't—

Don't forget

That they love you—

A sisterless sister—

A childless mom—

Listen to me,

Child—

You are the

Judge no more,

That time has

Passed—

Presents on a birthday—

Red lines on pure snow—

Turned black with

Guilt—red with

Raging anger.

They sit upon,

The patio,

And sing dirges

In the night—

A song of a

Seven-year-old—

In innocence

Did not know—

They sing dirges

In the night—

Yet, did I

Walk from that

Church, and did

Not know that

Because of you

Those dirges would

Hit so heavy—

For a friendless friend—

A sisterless brother—

They sit upon that

Patio, voices raised

For a young woman—

Whose voice will

Not speak, yet I

Hear her voice—

As she stands before

Me—

Stood before

Me—

I watched cartoons

With you—

And if only I'd known—

Back then—

To tell that seven-year-old—

Maybe—

You wouldn't—

Have hung yourself that day...

Paint the Leaves Red

Leaves of gray

A cat's claws

At the edges

Flay a man

So for the people—

They pray under

The steeple—

For the cat

To claw his

Back—that

He may bleed

Upon the world,

And cover it in

Red—

As Thomas stares

Through His hollow

Wrists and cries

Rabbi! Rabbi!

Why, you are

Who you claim!

The Muse Made Me Do It

Manic muse

O whisper to

Me—

And tell me

Tales I will not

Believe—

Sit upon my

Shoulder, shower

Me with wisdom

Mad and insane

O manic muse,

Love of my life

Grip my heart

And take my

Light—

Take me down

To the depths

Of hell, where

Only the darkest

Of stories they tell.

Show me a hero,

An innocent to

Save—a man

Who can rescue

The world from

The grave.

O manic muse,

You glorious maiden

You are my true

Love, against it

All forsaken.

Spyder on a Spindle

Spyder on a

Spindle—

Twisting away

Far from thought

Are the words

A wise man

Might say—

To the spyder

In the air—

Drifting here

And there.

A spyder on—

A spindle,

Twirling

Alive

Unaware

Of the

Grander things—

And destined

To die.

When the pigeon killed the whale

A pigeon from the

Hat to spear

The heart of

A wandering

Whale—soaring

Through the

Air—to sing

A song of

Freedom, to little

Avail—

He weeps—

He weeps—

Whilst the

Devil, well,

He sleeps,

And dreams

Of the rot

Of the world,

And feels

Hell's cold unfurled,

As Thomas hums

A song, and

Peter walks the

Waves alone—

But not afraid—

Not this time,

Doused in blood

And absolved of his crimes.

Walk the Moon

You walk

Into the moon

To find where

Thunder had

Hidden herself

From the

Heat of lightning's

Rod—spear

To scorch the

Earth like

The hammer

Of Thor

But she hides

Here now—

Inside the cold

Ashen moon,

And says

"My, my,

What a

Wondrous

World!"

I don't know if the rooster crowed

Crows once—

Crows twice—

And on the third

Judas cries—

To Peter's dismay

And John's discerning,

For neither sees

Their rabbi before

Them, yet they

Continue to eat

Fish—

4,000 before they

Grow full—

But it is too

Late—

Judas, don't

You see—

Everyone pays

In silver one day—

Crows once—

Crows twice—

And one day or

Another, all

Shall pay the price.

'Tis the fate

Of dust—

And dust alone—

For we are but naught

And ought to be gone.

If Moths Ate Lazarus

Large, it

Lays—and

The moth flies

Over the

Hill—

To the other

Side—

Apart from

When Lazarus

Died—

To fester

Upon the

Tomb—

To eat dying

Flesh.

Tell me, Lazarus,

What do you

Hear—across

The void that

Holds you dear?

To live again—

To sin again—

And a martyr

Is made—

Now sing a tune

In the tomb

Where you once laid.

Reading Seneca #1: To Nero

Seneca sat

Under the tree

And taught the

Mad Nero

To see—but

Far too fallen

Had the boy

Been, that

Death would

Rot his heart

In sin—

A heart of

Heat—devoid

Of love—

Power-hungry,

And never enough.

And lo! Before,

As Death sits at

The door, he mourns

Young Nero, now an old

Man—the wealthiest of

All—of kingdoms

Of sand.

Reading Seneca #2: Let's Be Happy

Breathe! Breathe!

You wonderful world!

Filled with injustice,

Yet beauty unfurled!

To the wiser things,

Metaphysical—

Lost and aspiring,

Musing whimsical—

The melody of

Life, the beauty

Of the tale of

Strife—

O! We want

To live! Beautiful

Away—and to

Time we give!

Perhaps! Perhaps!

Happiness is but

A sacrifice—

But a content day away.

Lilacs Lull for Lucy

Lilacs lull

Over Lucy's

Death—

Dead as

A door—

Nail in

The coffin—

O coffer

From which

The soul

From Purgatory

Shall spring—

Or whatever

It was that

Luther hated

So much,

And low

To the ground

She sinks

But the lilacs

Are pretty,

Or so it seems.

Under A Clockwork Sky

We waste

Our time, by

And by—

Sitting under

A falling

Sky, that

Grows closer

As we look—

Unaware of

The ticking

Clock—

As we watch

Our world

Fade away...

And lo! Do

We think,

As we sit

In the maybe:

My, my,

Time sure

Moves fast...

I knew Aurelius might say that…

A hand

If time—

Fleeting away,

Caught in

A spider's

Trap,

Or something

That Aurelius

Might say,

For we are

Always running

Our last lap,

So live your

Life with each

Present grain

Sifting through

The glass...

For all men's

Sake does Death

Await at the

Bottom of the

Hourglass.

Burning Time

Little and

Gone, slim

To the bone,

The world

Spins on

Its spindle,

Caught in

The cinders

Of burning

Time—

O, burning,

Burning time...

The Folly of Thomas

Thomas, Thomas,

You walked away

To the far wall

Only to hear what

It may say.

A journey you

Had, from the

Stone on the

Hill—far though

You still heard

The rabbi yell,

A yell of anguish—

A scream of love—

Caught between

The pain and

Reluctance that

Christ cried above...

But now you stand

Upon the sea sands

And you see that

All along—through

It all—for you,

For you—

Were the holes

Placed in His hands.

My Only Key

A lock—

Lost—

A trusted

Key

Who of all

Will say to

Me—the

Words I hear

The words I

Fear from

The ghosts

Who once loved me?

My fear

O dear

My beloved

Amid the

Nightmare—

Will you live

And lie with me?

And show me you

Are true?

Because,

I want to believe;

I want to believe;

Only because you are you.

Prayer #1

Create in

Me, something

Good and pure,

O Lord of

All, make

Me new.

Cling to

The Blood, I

Will—I will

Follow the

Road taken

By the few.

Resurrect in

Me, the Spirit;

Cover me in

His blood, and

Give me strength

Today, to live as

He would.

His blood, and

Give me strength

Today, to live as

He would.

The Owl Hymn

A dream

Dreamed of

Simple things

Beyond a pastel

Veil, he sits

Among the

Beautiful ashes

And laughs to

No avail.

The dark

Does not

Blind him

In his vehement

Reverie, cured

By an owl's hymn

From some distant

Tree.

For the grandest

Things are

Not found in

Glory or gold,

But in the simplest

Times, passing and

Growing old, for he

Sits there, his chains

Gone, and now set

Free, and laughs aloud,

"O! Owl, keep singing to me!"

The Failure Poem

Pictures

Upon

A fractured stage

In flames of moths

And rust,

I reach out

To touch the

Sun, but

Forget that I am

Dust

Lost in sorrow

Of happy times

In glimpses of

Glee found in

The light that slips

Through

I see you now

What you've become

And I wonder if

There was anything I

Could Have

Done

My friend

My friend

I'm sorry I

Hung up the

Phone

Please, O!

Please don't

Leave so soon

Into abyss where

The rest of my

Things hide

In a lock fastened

By a key of lies

But I guess I

Should say

I'm sorry to myself

For I am all

Who I have failed...

Cast A Lot (it's not so bad)

Severed

Selves

A great divide

Casts a lot for

The clothes

Of wasted time,

I see, I saw

An unraveled

Seems, lost

Within, a siren

Sings,

An ode to here

Of ire and ruin

To be secondary

To a life too

Soon,

Too long, to

Wield a

Severed spike,

And rapture to

An end delight

So I sit here now,

I shake, I sing,

And I know again

There is an end

To all bad things.

The Kitty Poem

Kitty, kitty,

I see you more

through the

heart and in

the door—

Kitty, kitty,

may it not be

this way, that

over there I might

see, beyond the

chasm of you and

me, that you might be,

for just a moment...

content and asleep...

O, little kitty, sleep.

Tarnished Gold (A Ransom Sold)

A lost

Alone,

The sky

Calls home,

Of rivers deep

And lonesome

Souls, we give

Our hearts, a

Ransom sold

From here to

There, a star

Disappears,

Though light

May shine, its

History, I

Sing a song

From you to

Me — I

Love you, dear,

That I do, and I'm

Sorry that I am

A deafened tune

Of false and fake,

Beneath the lake,

Of lies and desired

Truth...

I love you dear, though

I cannot show, for

Lost am I, tarnished gold.

To No [Avail]

Life beyond a

Thin lit veil, a cost,

A ward to kiss the

Tale—the world we

See by the midnight's

Naught—a vestige, free

And carries what

We see, we see, and all

Must tell,

For in the end,

There was no avail.

All but Everything

A glass of

Sorts, beyond the

Door, where moonlight

Sings her end,

A piece of life

And justice or

Some lost and

Lonely thing.

We sit here,

Now, above the

Bow, and hear a

Raven sing,

But unto here,

And heaven's glare, is

All but everything.

Bedside Death

Eyed,

A lark

In distant dreams

Of meter. You

Sit among the

Life of things

And the verges of there

And here

A lost man

Cries

Out to you by

Night

But in the day

A baby lies

And fibs within

  WILLIAM F. BURK

The light

O man,

Morose man,

What lost are

Your own rights?

You bed among the

Grove of thorns

With Death by

Your bedside.

C-PTSD

Ashes cast

Upon a field

That dies with

Everything,

A locket

Tied around my

Waist, that swears

He loves me,

A lash upon

A lark's dead

Wings, lost in

Leather—beaten

Things.

I see

I saw

A man's dead

Heart, a beating

Now, may start

The dreaded thing,

In a field,

Away from everything.

Empathy is, a quiet

Voice, lost to those,

Lost to me,

A jealous man,

Swears he loves

Me, but denies my

Heart, my everything.

Innocent—

Helpless—

How could he

Love me?

For scars upon

A broken child

Defy any love

You claim to

Be.

La Viva Mar

A tear

Into

La viva mar

A madman croaks

The view, of

Little things—

Those left behind,

And everything

In between.

A shade of

Light, a beacon

Still, in every

Small domain

I sit here now

And watch we

Swing, and sing

Along to the

Rest of me.

Poem #J

Mist

Upon

The

Mountain

Air

Midst

The

Sorrow

Down

Sings

Praises

To

The

Moon

Above

That

Lights

The

Morose

Ground.

Astray

Loss is

Lots of laughter

Gone, spent

In morning

Days,

A life of

Love and

Meager then,

A mourning

Beneath the

Haze

We find when

We, sit there

Too, and wonder

Where we've been

A time or two,

We lost the

Pen, to write

Our fates away.

In ink and sea,

Our lives are

Fleeting still,

And in the end,

To dust we be

And must

All but all

Decay.

Sing to me,

Sing your soul,

We die at the

End of days,

And think, O,

Dust, what could

You be, but for

The winds to

Blow astray.

Liar's Whispering Wrongdoings Wrought

What are you

Really

Show me your

Face, despised and

Haunted unholy

Grace

Devourer of

Pain, like sweetened

Milk, to see the

Face, show me

That face that

Was struck

Do you see

What you are, lost

Beneath

The pieces of

Me? Sickening

Angel, speaking

Sweet, and tell me the

World wants to

Eat me whole

I hear you now

I tune you out

For I can see now

You are simply lying.

No One Can Tell

A place

Beyond

A moonlit

Veil, begone

Of places that

None can tell.

The Distant/Window

A saw

before

a fractured

tell, beyond

the word and

world did meld,

and see the things

that came to pass,

guided by all at

last. To see, to sing

led through a prayer, lost

beyond, a midnight

glare, of the

moon on

high, I do not

see, the distance

between you, and

the window to me.

My Socials and Website

FACEBOOK: @burkwillwrites

X/TWITTER: @BurkWill

INSTAGRAM: @williamfburk.author

YOUTUBE: @WilliamFBurk

TIKTOK: @burkwillwrites

www.williamfburk.com